Release From Darkness

- Words For Spring -

Poetry for all Seasons
Ana Lisa de Jong

Humanities
ACADEMIC PUBLISHERS

Hardcover: 978-1-98-855775-5
Softcover: 978-1-98-855776-2
Ebook: 978-1-98-855777-9

Published in New Zealand

A catalogue record for this book is available from the National Library of New Zealand.

Kei te pātengi raraunga o Te Puna Mātauranga o Aotearoa te whakarārangi o tēnei pukapuka.

Table of Contents

'I mourned, and yet shall mourn
with ever-returning spring.'

— Walt Whitman

Introduction

The last lines of my very last poem in this collection read 'So let us come singing, remembering who we are – branches of the vine bearing spring to one another'.

What does it mean to remember who we are, and how do we remember in the midst of winter? How do we pick up our seeds, prepare the earth, and scatter them out on our tilled soil to then water and wait for something to grow?

I imagine it comes from believing in the power of a seed and a bed of loam to do wonders – or of having seen and believed, so that we can then believe to see again.

Which is what spring repeats each coming year, this glorious act of growing. And the knowledge that spring is always coming, and always repeatable, no matter the travails of winter, provides a foundation, a fertile bed for our faith.

So, faith is as much born of remembrance as of hope. And hope is not just the imagination of things possible, but the assurance of things probable – borne out by history's testimony. We have been here before, in the winter, and the spring has returned.

We have been here sorrowing, been here in a bleak desert, a dark depression, in a season devoid of colour or life – whatever has weighed us down, left us just holding on through the winter – we can start to feel it lift in the gentle stirrings of spring, the eternal leaning towards life that spring portrays.

Another stanza in the same poem reads, *'let us coming loving, forgetting what we are not, for griefs do not define us and joy responds to joy'.*

'Joy responding to joy' when we relate to spring might be considered to be in the way life begets life, how stirrings soon become a flourish of growing, a celebratory communion together.

And 'griefs not defining us' leads us back to the title of this book, *Release from Darkness – Words for Spring.* The title of which, like the other books in this seasonal series, is based upon Isaiah 61, the prophecy of Isaiah concerning the Messiah. Reading Isaiah 61 again, I notice how the promise is in how what we have experienced up to now is to be replaced by its exact opposite: *'a crown of beauty instead of ashes, the oil of joy instead of mourning, and a garment of praise instead of a spirit of despair'.*

And spring itself does a kind of turnaround, a full circle from winter and its deprivation of life. And release for us, perhaps, is not in fully forgetting, but it is laying down our bondages, stepping out of the ties that have bound us, and like the plant re-emerging from the garden bed, stretching fully up to a warming sun.

Ana Lisa de Jong
Living Tree Poetry
December 2020

The Vine

God is a God who waits
with all things new.

The vine soaks in the morning sun.
The sap stirs and runs.
We are here attached.
The one who was promised
has come, has not left.

It is we who feel a quickening
to an ever-giving love.
We feel the sun,
our blood, our skin sings
in the life in which we live –
connected.

That we are alone
is not a truth that stands
to the light,
but dissolves as mist in sun,
is absorbed in running sap.

Joy's Face

I want to write of joy

but not the joy that parades,
the joy that needs bells and whistles,
occasions.

I want to write of joy

that arrives in every season,
that undergirds all the fleeting feelings
arising.

I want to write of joy

but not of the overblown rose with
her scents and opulence,
her full-headed extravagance –

but of something small,
simple, unassuming,
bashful even in its graciousness.

I want to write of the joy

that ever goes unnoticed
for its ordinariness,
the sight of it common as the grass, the trees.

This is the joy that, when asked
to measure our days, we will recognise
as the underlying feature

as common as the daisies
lifting their bright heads.

March 2 - Northern Hemisphere
September 2 - Southern Hemisphere

Grass

Three of the most beautiful lines:

'He does not raise his voice;
He does not crush the weak,
or quench the smallest hope.'

So all our hopes,
though they might beat against our chest with wings
or lie smaller than a mustard seed
hidden in the hand,
can grow in time
like the tall grass lengthening.

Can incline towards faith
as seedlings seek out the light,
surpassing themselves
with the warmth of the sun
and the wind
speaking over them.

Mary Oliver speaks of the catbird,
'common as the grass',
who has picked his pond and made
a soft thicket of the world –

that in wonderment I consider
how good it really is

to be one of many
in an ever-stirring, breathing
mass of humanity.
Perhaps not so different
to a kingdom measured out in the grass
from fencepost to gate,

the breeze gently whispering,
the soft sun delivering a steady coverage.

Your Countenance

Will you think of me
when you come to set your jewels?

I am tarnished and worn,
I am nothing beyond the skin
illuminated in your gaze.

And where your rays cannot find me,
I am a deep cavern of want
and shadows.

That your light in which I try to raise
my face
must become more than day to me,

must reach me here in the night,
the places I go to hide.

Must make my darkness so bright
that even shadows run
from your appearance.

And then, maybe, I might
become the gem that bears the fire
in which I'm held.

Your countenance turned toward me,
this gaze of yours
that seeks me out.

Untold Ways

I would like to write
like a violin's note
stretching out into infinity.

Giving space in a moment
for a thousand different impressions.

I would like to write
as a dancer steps,
weaving a magic spell.

Giving rise to all the emotions
that a moment holds.

I would like to write
like water falls
in a million droplets off the edge.

And then, I would like to plummet
with the strength of an ocean behind.

I would like to write
with music leading,
muse through the forest,

cutting in and out,
seeing that I follow.

And I would like to write
with the voice in me you've given,
echoing as your name does

in countless untold ways.

March 5 - Northern Hemisphere
September 5 - Southern Hemisphere

Balancing

It's a long, slow progression into the day.

A balancing act,
like shifting our weight from one foot to the other,

to choose the thoughts we'll follow.

It's possible to see a thing two ways,
or a myriad more even,

sometimes it's a weighing and discarding
of a thing that doesn't further.

Sometimes it's choosing what we see,
in the knowledge that its imprint matters.

So my ritual, in this long, slow procession,
is to focus in

at the hydrangeas unfolded as I slept,
and the wild blue iris,

scene changing with the roses
fading out.

Perhaps to miss these things would be akin
to arriving at church after worship.

So, knowing how it all matters to the psyche,
my soul and I decide the thoughts the mind will follow.

And then proceed,

we, as beggars starved for goodness,
collecting crumbs left by the angels on the road.

Beauty

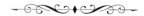

Ah, beauty is beckoning us.

And for all her glorious tresses,
her unguarded, open face,
her generous, voluptuous gift,
beauty is shy and retiring,
uneager to draw a crowd,
more often sneaking up unawares
with something singularly unique.

So that when we partake of her gift,
beauty is surprisingly intimate,
personally present
in a way that speaks of her
being prepared,
seeking our acquiescence,
bidding our attentiveness.

Yes, there is something about
the undressed face
of a beauty unadorned
that returns us to childhood complete,
to innocence again without question
or doubt,
as infants expectant of grace.

It's as though she wordless states,
'You think the world has turned,
but I am full circle,
come about,
find me where you began.'

March 7 - Northern Hemisphere
September 7 - Southern Hemisphere

Watching for the Morning

I am a watchperson for the morning.

Up there
in the wind's domain,
the clouds move as passing ships,
their grey giving way to silver blue,
to white,
at the touch of sun.

What seems ominous
from a distance
meets the light
and changes hue,
becomes transparent,
is all of a sudden overcome.

Revealed as such things
as they have always been,
although we,
with the light behind us,
perceive them first
as shadows growing.

Do not know
how in the sun

they will dissolve, garments shed,
the things that rendered them fearful
invisible now
to the eye.

Their remnants shrinking,
their essence remaining
to make me think,
watchperson for the morning,
that everything in God
that is not transformed,

that cannot stand up to the light,
bows out,

bows out.

March 8 - Northern Hemisphere
September 8 - Southern Hemisphere

The Birds

If I could send the birds today
to speak to you,
to share my heart,

I would ask for the joyous
songs of the fantail
to lift your spirit.

For the kereru's call
to fill and tenderly
woo you.

And the tui's clear notes
to strike a chord
at your heart's core.

I would ask,
that you might pause and
close your eyes

and hear the notes
you've heard many a night
and morning

but with such a clarity
you'll no longer wonder
if it's the language of heaven –

but will know for sure.

Know that church bells
can never match
nature's voice.

Nor angels sing with such
a lilting ring as the smallest
songbird.

Yes, I will ask for the
humble sparrow to teach you
the truth about heaven.

It's already here for those
who hear its call.

Your Will

What if we could say to you, 'your will be done'?
Not our will – well thought out, dreamed and hoped –
but yours.

I wonder who can say that easily?
Without hesitation, without withholding
all the things we would keep your hands from holding.

How is it we will learn to trust, to believe
that anything you have for us is better than
the things we seek to keep.

Is it that we are too ready to connect
the loss of will with a garden in Gethsemane,
that to give such a vow entails surrendering,

a giving in to suffering
that we feel ourselves, in our human shells,
ill equipped to bear, receive?

This cup that arrives full, emptying.

Yes, perhaps we need to reimagine
the concept of giving in, submitting,
and forget the courage we think we need.

The holiness we need to gain
and wear as a cloak to shield us from the
world's dirt, its unending diversions.

Maybe your will is instead an invitation,
a wild wooing of the heart into partnership
with our soul's beloved, its central core.

Yes, what is your will but a one-way street,
a communing, a melding of the self
into the greater force of two.

What if we could say to you, 'your will be done in me'?
Not my will, my insufficient hopes and dreams,
my griefs and pinings,

but everything you want for me,
the path you would prepare.

March 10 - Northern Hemisphere
September 10 - Southern Hemisphere

Signals

My morning prayer rises
with the light.
Swells like the billowing bud
or the ocean's wave
against a shore.

Crests like the sun
edging over the hill,
catching the light,
each bark and leaf
turned to its glow.

My morning prayer escapes
as breath
meeting the cool dawn air,
or as birds suspended
in the pleasure of flight

and wraps me
as pink,
apricot clouds,
enveloping the sun,
foretelling the day's coming.

My morning prayer echoes
without a word
across the plains, hills
and vales,
above the oceans.

To meet the one
who sends it back
in the billowing bud,
the sun's display,
the day's arrival.

Like a signal
to confirm the hearing,
or a sign of affirmation.
As a beacon might shine
from a lighthouse on a hill.

Blooming

I want to be like the flower,
rooted.

Who has seen a flower
that has fought its bloom,

has wished itself
not to grow.

Who has seen a flower
that has not had everything

come to it,

though it has stayed rooted
in place.

Has not seen the wind,
the sun,

all the seasons
visit in turn.

Yes, I want to be like the flower,

not wishing to be anywhere
different.

But rooted here,

opening wide
at the bud.

Grace

Everyone dreams of a love
that comes to find them.
Pursues them down.
Pries the heart and carefully undoes them.

Everyone is human,
and love a precursor to our sanctifying.
While we dream of gentle saviours,
love is an instrument bent on mining

and hollowing out the heart to
greater depths, that instead
of sudden comings, our saviour
is a seed sown.

And while we seek a healer
or rider on the horizon,
God plants himself as
a diamond laid down in the rough.

Yes, everyone dreams of a love
that arrives for us,
with intimate knowledge that
we need no pretence or argument.

But in the ways we receive
and fail to give grace,
love is doing its silent growing
inside of us.

March 13 - Northern Hemisphere
September 13 - Southern Hemisphere

Saved

I don't think I want to be saved today.
Not from myself, or the world.

What great blessings might we bestow
if we called out the intrinsic nugget of self.

If we leaned over one another
whispering, 'grow, grow.'

Is it only 'the saved' who inherit
the kingdom?

What does it mean to follow the light?

Imagine,

if we were not so much containers of sin
as vessels of immeasurable value.

Both/And

from the beginning.

Such that the little God lights
lit at birth were fanned into flames

by us each receiving each other
as gifts from heaven.

I know the birds don't need to renounce their being
and be remade part way in.

And are we not creatures then,
like them?

Ah yes, I like to think I came with life already lodged
deep in the heart,

and in the living
God has stretched out and made a home.

March 14 - Northern Hemisphere
September 14 - Southern Hemisphere

Saved II

Yesterday I didn't want to be saved,

which is my way of saying
I didn't want the naysayers to win.

I didn't want a name defined
by weakness.

Sinner. Sin.

But today,
today salvation takes on
a different meaning.

Which is how it works, doesn't it?
The Living Word.

The unchanging script,
which speaks still in ways we've not yet heard.

Which enables us to believe

and not throw out the bath
with the water it contains.

And so yesterday
I didn't want to be saved.

But today it provides the softest landing.

A bit like a father who always believes
no matter what anyone else has heard.

A father who says,

'Now, my created,
you are yet to discover your real name.'

Yes, can you imagine being loved
even a little bit

like that?

Even a fraction of such love,
enough for us to lift our heads,

face the world again.

March 15 - Northern Hemisphere
September 15 - Southern Hemisphere

Hope's Disappearance

Did hope disappear,
rush ahead,
turn the corner,
leave us here?

Did hope,
while we slept,
roll over, departing
before daybreak?

Did hope quit,
give up on us,
decide we were no good,
not enough?

Did hope
change,
become someone we never knew,
let us down?

Did hope
put on his backpack,
cut his bets,
hit the road —
not look back?

Or did hope
fail himself,
deciding we'd be better off
for his absence?

Did hope
forget,
turn the corner,
cast us far from mind?

Did hope
run ahead,
round the bend,
forsake us here?

Did hope
take time to leave a trail,
a clue to study,
something to follow?

Or did hope
disintegrate,
like clouds turned dark,
to block the sun?

Did hope know
we would not understand,
did hope speak a language
we couldn't attempt to learn?

And did hope act out,
to demonstrate
instead
what we couldn't comprehend?

Did love lie down,
did love break his heart,
pouring it open,
to bring us his love?

Did hope disappear,
or did love for a moment
shield his face,
to turn it back to us

illuminated.

Dawning Light

Ah, when the heart is too deeply grieved,
sometimes the light is too bright a thing.

The hurt animal seeks a dark habitat to
hide.

Perhaps it's safety that is perceived
in the half light.

Perhaps it is the same as wearing black
in mourning,

in that once there was apportioned a time to
rightly grieve.

Now, even grief is a thing
we must examine in the shade.

The light can't be tarnished by a people
casting shadows.

Ah, but when the heart is deeply grieved
light comes gently.

At first a sliver through the curtains
left a chink or two open.

And then, once we can bear it,
a sun beam cast upon the floor.

When we see the light will only shine
where we can receive it,

we will trust the way
it can illuminate our path.

The light with tender knowing
will not show us much up front,

so that we might just see our way
to the turn in the road.

Yes, all the garish light bearers
have long missed the point.

The light dawns slowly
as sunlight traverses the hill.

March 17 - Northern Hemisphere
September 17 - Southern Hemisphere

Suspended

There are so many things that keep us abreast,
that can lift us and carry us through.

Today for me,
it was the long note of a tune
suspended in the light

and the way one note followed the other
as waves do upon a beach,
constant and consistent.

Yes, one friend talks about the way
we can always begin,

that as children of the resurrection
everything is new
and grace a door forever open.

So today I sing
and watch how a note will carry on and on
until it's done

and another then enters
from the wings.

March 18 - Northern Hemisphere
September 18 - Southern Hemisphere

Waiting

There's much talk about finding heaven here,
and then again, we know this as a waiting room.

Sometimes I feel like a bride
trying on her wedding clothes.

What else but anticipation is felt in the spring sunshine
under the apple blossoms?

Other times, I fight to be worthy of myself
and waiting seems a long walk.

And heaven less of an expectation
than a nostalgic reminiscence.

As though we come with half a heart
to spend our lives seeking connections.

But I rein in such thoughts,
for what gift is this

that stares me in the face
in a pre-taste of the banquet?

If this is wooing, then I am already undone,
deep in love –

so many signals from the bridegroom.

Not least our earthly passions
and blessings,

and an earth that brings our jaws
to the ground.
There is fulfilment and awe here,
but in such brief concentrated bursts
that it's as though the more we have
the more we're left wanting.

Too soon the sun sets behind the pines,
the wind cools,

we are left reminded of the four walls
of this waiting house.
That today I sit here in my imagination
smoothing down white satin folds,
this apple blossom confetti,
birdsong like wedding bells.

A Garden in my Thoughts

Maybe there is a garden in my thoughts.

I know my soul,
in deciding what to do,

will follow the way of light
through the trees,
will seek the singing bird.

Will kneel in the loam and
thank the fallow earth for seeds,
trust the winds.

Yes, there is a garden in my thoughts.
And I learn the seasons
by watching the leaves.

There is no noise
but the breeze brushing the foliage,
the bird's call,

its forage for food amongst leaf mulch,
the rustling of the
earthen floor.

And I realise everything is here,
death, birth,
the spaciousness of life.

The rooted things
that remind us to plant ourselves,
branch out to a shape defined

by who we are,
the replication of cells,
the grace gift, enough.

The pattern of leaves,
and the direction of veins –
a path to follow from root to tip.
And the singing bird,
making a home in the universe.

There is a garden in my thoughts.

Yes to Surrender

What does it mean to say Yes?
Part of me is afraid

that Yes is a leap,
a large wide open 'Y',
a stretch of muscle and limb,
a reach in each direction,
that Yes looks more like
a fall, a deep, wide-open abyss.

But, what does it mean to say Yes?
Perhaps God is reflected in

the way I've watched,
from winter to spring,
the self-seeded bulbs
warming in the earth,
sending their green spheres up
as though testing the temperature
before endeavouring forth.

And perhaps Yes starts to look
like a river's passage,

where white water is less
of a choice than a ride,
carrying us on its wave
with nary a backwards look,
like the flowers taking shape
on the tip of a shoot,
still tight,

warming up.

'And Mary said, "Behold, I am the servant of the Lord;
let it be to me according to your word."'
Luke 1:38

March 21 – Northern Hemisphere
September 21 – Southern Hemisphere

A New Thing

Ah, God does a new thing
and tells us not to worry.

He tries to tell us in the
rounding sun,
the dark chased away.

And if we doubt,

he tells us in the recurring themes
of restoration,

the cycles of the days
and seasons.

I know I get up early
in the dark,

ruminating,

thinking it's still yesterday.

And God sits me down
with his Word,

like a sun just risen.

A shoreline washed
by the tide.

Dumb

While the earth is still breathing
I will listen to her heart beat.
She has things to share in the wind's breath,

and while the sun turns
I will pivot like the plants
towards her face.

Yes, I am aware I say too much.

But don't we each create a life
from which we preach
in pulpits of our making?

And then, step outside
struck dumb by the eloquence
of a language without speech.

We hear the birds in the trees,
their songs clear and succinct
in praise and thanks.

We sit in a short few inches,
and the grass moves with life
that we jump to our feet.

Yes, in all of our advancements
we find ourselves surpassed
yet again

by the creatures living in balance
with the earth.

Between Us

Don't you know,
don't we know
what lies in our hands?

A planet, round.
What we touch each
resonating to the
other side.

Can you feel the tremble
of the green tree
in leaf,

from the wind that
passed by
on its turning circle?

A planet, round.
Where I stand,
you kneel to feel,

and I am aware
of how the foliage
falling,

a discarded robe,
is collected up
and donned anew

in your
greening spring
returning.

Don't we know?
Yes, don't we see
what lies beating.

A land to have,
to hold, to cherish,
something shared.

Don't we see
what lies solid,
a living being breathing,

held fast
between us,
this planet round,

that links your hand in mine.

March 24 – Northern Hemisphere
September 24 – Southern Hemisphere

God Appearing

And God came down,
said he would appear when we least expected.

And God came here,
slipping in behind a door left open.

Appearing like an angel bearing gifts.

And we were too fearful
to believe,

too blind to see,
restless for peace,

too anxious to trust the darkness
easing,

shifting its dark wings,
its swirling skirts.

As we,
locked into a corner,

felt the great crevice of separateness widening,
opening underneath.

Yes, into this God appeared,

timed his arriving to when
we might be most in need,

most lost,
in all the ways we had failed to live

and save ourselves.

And like with Lazarus,
God drew in,

first crying for the knowledge of
our losses

and then turning to the business at hand

of raising the dead,

of placing us upon our feet
again,

hope filled and
expectant.

Brief

I wonder why it is that spring must blossom,
must erupt in company with the wind.

Why it is that a bud would form,
as fragile as tissue,
unfold and compete with a gust.

Why it is the sweet things are brief
and the longest length in waiting
for things that are gone in a breath.

Why it is that beauty loves to dance,
though she must drop her garments
and then fall like a leaf to the ground.

I wonder why the hope that this year
the trees will carry their crowns
under a balmy spring, summer sky.

As though spring isn't a mix of winter
and something
that looks strangely like hope without restraints.

Let free without thought,
as though for this it were made,
a fling, a flourish, a give way.

Clothed

Grief wears such warm clothes.
The warmth of love remembered.
The warmth of memories.
It's just, it's cold where the clothes let in the wind.
Under the cuffs. Inside the collar.
Beneath the shirt hem.
It's like the grave freshly covered,
the blossom on the overhanging shrub.
Everything's so beautiful under the sky blue,
the daffodils in a glass jar,
the exquisite tender feeling.
But then you remember,
in a sudden chill of wind,
that you're bereft of that person now
six feet under.
They can't share this.
You can't share them.

Mahi

My friend takes thread and embroiders with it,
each stitch an act of love.

I can take a word
and sit
and watch it grow.

Who would have imagined
the poetry in it.

Others might see an idle moment
an absorption inconsistent
with life's constant current.

I say, what is life
but the seed,
the creative ebb and flow.

My friend makes beauty stitch by stitch.

Inhabits the hours
and the minutes,
impregnates them with holy intent.

Though she might not know it
as sacred attention,

absorbed as she is
in her task.

At Home

When I am home
in a quiet capsule,

I can feel isolated,
quarantined.

Though I might have a door, a street,
a means of travel,

I can still feel small,
unseen, unknown.

How to know
that sitting can make a difference,

with silence echoing,
a child's laughter distant,

intercepted by
a cold spring wind.

Yes, when I am home in
a quiet capsule,

it helps to know
I am here observed,

accompanied and surrounded
by the unseen attending,

keeping me in
their intimate fold.

Amazing

It's amazing that you saw me,
conceived of me, before I was a cell dividing,
an embryo, a being.

Where do you do your imagining, God?

Is there a pond you gaze upon
whose colours turn to shapes
to signify the flesh, the face?

Is that where you decide?

Or is it that you see us in the back of your eyes,
lids closed,
thinking how you'd feel to know your love redirected,

to be the focus of another's heart?

It's amazing that you see us,
believe in us,
even when we falter, fail,

remain as clay.

Is there a point passed
where you dismiss us, are insulted,
push the canvas aside,

want instead a different shape, heart, face?

It's amazing that you see us, God,
conceive of us, before we are a cell dividing,
an embryo, a being.

Before we spring from nothing.

It's more amazing that you trust

in the fulfilment of your redemption.
That in your eyes is seen
nothing more than our own reflection,

smiling, taking shape.

Budding

I'm going to tell you a secret
as clear as the sunrise,
the one that shakes you awake each day.

I'm going to say –
like the flower bud that draws the bees –
that perhaps you were placed,
desired,
formed like a bud unfolding,
to be at the end of the stem,
the focus of God's gaze.

Perhaps God made you
for no great purpose other
than to love you with
intimate attentiveness,
and perhaps the best gift God claims back
is the love you give yourself
in turn.

Within that,
purpose blossoming,
fruiting,
as the flowering shrub
in spring bloom.

Affirmation
– on the touch of a therapist

I met a woman today who told me about
my body.

I thought I knew it well,
but she showed me how
it responded to the things within,
without –

the intricacy of muscle and organ,
the mechanisms that work
without thought,
to serve so graciously, quietly.

And she showed me how
one could love it back to wholeness
when it's tired, or confused,
how its strength was to be honoured.

This body borne, a part of us.
Not just sinew and bone,
flesh and skin,
born to do our bidding –

but the very core of thought,
of feeling, action and intent –
the spiritual well of life,
the fire glowing in our midst.

And she showed me how
I could tend to it deep,
breathe into its hallowed depths,
bring it to the forefront.

Give it its own valid space,
permission to spread,
flex its wings, fill its place,
belong.

Our sense of safety
bound so tight with springs
held fixed in tension's grasp,
dependent on surviving –

could yet find release
in the relaxing of muscles,
the breathing in and out –
the marrying of self to breath.

Could succumb fully to pain's relief,
in the permission given itself
to exist,
to live.

The Sweet Spot

I have a sweet spot.
It's in the centre of a poem,
threads coming together
in the mystery of unfolding.

There's the wait,
breath in and breath out,
an awareness like antennae
combing the airwaves.

It's like standing on a precipice,
the edge before the jump,
where the winds meet.
It's like being in prayer.

And the free fall,
a plunge with the heart wide open,
like a parachute taking us slow
across a valley.

We each have our sweet spots
in the centre of the mystery,
giving us a glimpse to make
the breath inhale,

and then release of
the long out breath –
like making love.
Yes, we all have our thing

in which the particles in us shiver to life.
The place in which all of life is,
for a moment,
held suspended.

And we then both succumb
and dive in,
stand tall and astride,
a bit like a surfer catching the crest of the wave.

Two of Us

If there are two of me,
one is running up the hill.

The other can be heard to say,
'Slow down, you're not as good at this
as you pretend.'

This thing called life
that calls us to the peaks of experience.

But, thank goodness, there are two of me.

One to pack the sunblock
and the bandaids,
to count the funds.

And the other to dream,
to venture in, heedlessly.

Yes, if there are two of me,
one is not measuring ability.

The other can be heard to say,
'What do you bring, what makes you
have a word to say?'

'And watch out, you are prone to trip,
to drive into accidents.'

But the other
has a way of brushing off warnings
as irritants in the road.

Life that can't be stopped has a voice
to which we never come qualified.

But the hearing has a way of awakening
in us a thousand possibilities –
that if there are two of us,

one is running up ahead.

Beauty As Bread

We need beauty as much as bread.
Perhaps, in a sense,
beauty is its own form of bread.
One we do not arrive at hungry again.

But a kind of bread that sustains.
Nourishes, that the smallest morsel
can shine as a jewel against the dark,
can make all our days.

What is a room with shutters closed
compared to an open arched
window framed, revealing how
the humblest view can widen our vision.

And what is beauty but
a singular type of promise,
potential distilled to its most basic,
invigorating essence.

A kind of boundless optimism.
Beauty, just because.
Because in a seed, in an ear of wheat,
is all its grain.

No wonder we are filled.

After the Rains

After the rains the sun comes,
after the night is dawn.
After labour is rest,
after the climb is the view.

After,
everything comes after.
It's as though after is a gate,
a fence behind which blessing is stored.

But before,
before is a long blank space.
A desert or a wilderness,
a necessary ascent.

Before is a question mark
or an aching absence,
it's the fresh mark of mistakes,
the sweat of toil.

But after is a storm hushed,
a mother's soft lullaby.
The hands of nurses at our beds
in the still pre-dawn dark.

After is a long recovery,
an outgoing breath and inhale,
an awakening to knowledge,
a forgiveness and a grace.

After is a healing,
with an emphasis on time.
We have redeemed now the year's ended,
and have time now for everything.

And after is the release,
when the worked muscles rest.
The moment when the open 'Why'
becomes an 'O' of understanding.

Or if not, becomes something
we can accept.
And after is the view,
how it astounds in its expansiveness.

And we think how grown the world is now,
how green after the rains end.

Something New

The world asks something of us each moment.

Sometimes it's so hard to offer up,
it's like the breaking of a husk.

And sometimes it's easy
as falling snow, sunlight.

Sometimes it feels like giving up,
giving in,

floating without support,
standing on a precipice.

Other times, it's as possible as
being made for this moment,

this very thing.

Yet again,

the moments that wring us out
and spin us,

to drop us from their heights –
these are the ones

which, like the breaking of a husk
to bring something forth,

make something new of us,
something else again.

There Comes a Day

There comes a day when
it no longer matters what others think.

All that matters now
is that we follow our own lead.

That we no longer resist
the urge to get our feet wet.

At the waterside.
At the harbour, where we draw our own tide.

Yes, all that matters now
is that we source the depths of our own longing.

For we know that our very being depends
on the truths we tell ourselves.

And these truths are reflected now
in the stillness of the water's surface.

Yes, look and find
that after all, you are perfect.

To your own self to which you are now true.
And to your own purposes which call you.

April 7 – Northern Hemisphere
October 8 – Southern Hemisphere

Linings

If you can't see a silver lining,
turn things inside out.

Wash them with hope-filled abandon,
hang them in the sun.

Let the wind whip them loose and
release them of their weights.

Gather them dry and soft,
hold them close to heart.

Place your face deep in
and smell the residue of breeze.

And see how the sunlight
has left its mark

in a silver-threaded hem.

To Love the Unlovely

Remember everyone grew
wanting to be lovely,
talented,
complete,
without the ache of need,
the fear of lack,
the spectre of inadequacy.

And to every seed that grew,
there was a space shaped
for it to branch out into,
spread and fill
with the hope of growth,
the expectation of return,
a trust in fruit.

And for every heart formed
there was bone and sinew,
muscle,
strength developed,
a frame to contain a beating core,
hands and feet,
legs to propel.

And a mind imagining,
unarmed,
unconscious of threat,
of coming hurt,
pregnant with possibility,
ripening potential,
believing yet.

And everyone grew
wanting to be lovely,
talented,
complete,
without the shock of loss,
the sting of shame,
the erosion of esteem.

Remember everyone grew
with hope beating
out a silent rhythm,
a song-sheet to sing.
That when it's hard to love
we remember
the song,

we remember the seed.

Threads

This wisdom from above
is that everything is enclosed
in one round circle.

Does it matter where
we start or end,
finish up?

No, I think it matters
more that we begin.

The thread we pick up
just another in a web
that was fully formed before us.

What do we add?

Perhaps God in his grace
loans us a part to play for our growth.

Magnanimously giving us the gift of
ownership,
however badly we trip up.

But really there are no rules,
just this great wide web,
lit here,

shining in the sun.

April 10 - Northern Hemisphere
October 11 - Southern Hemisphere

A Wick

My friend asked me where I find God.
There is so much everywhere,
I must exhale deep and breathe in that God
might travel down.

Past the sternum, further in.
The breath that's not my own,
until the spreading peace is like the
sky in the morning sun.

Yes, God that is like oxygen
shows how this presence fills.
It's in the way the hill's
tree-lined crest is a wick set to light with gold.

April 11 – Northern Hemisphere
October 12 – Southern Hemisphere

Look See

Look at this.
You are beautiful.
Yes! You!

For you have a heart beating
and a mind capable of thought,
of feeling.
A soul in tune with eternity.

And a smile,
a face to see,
with two eyes
to look back at me.

If we both see each other
as beautiful,
then right here,
in this place

there is nothing but
beauty.
Look and see.

New Leaves

Death and life, I think we choose each day.
That defeat is not so much an enemy
as a parent, a friend endorsing us to
raise our heads,
opening the curtains by our beds,
speaking of newness.

And life,
sometimes it fully unravels by night time
and the only thing to stop us tossing and despairing in our sleep,
or attempts at it,
is the promise of the light returning.

And death, death is often that moment
in the water we've outswam our endurance
and begun to sink,
until our bursting lungs find relief from a lifeline tossed,
a re-emergence on the surface.

And whoever saw a shoreline so very beautiful
as those who thought they wouldn't again
feel sand underfoot, or receive
the welcome of a lightening dawn,
or turn over a new leaf

in spring.

Identity

Who are you afraid of?
Could it be your beauty can slay dragons?

Perhaps the world asks you to hide away your light
because it's the very thing
that harbours magic.

For everyone's a bit in awe
of the ones that don't
water down their colours.

The ones that look in the mirror
and encourage themselves
to life.

The ones that do not stop to
question their reflection,

the light they follow
so luminous,

shed from the love
they cast.

A Box

Every mother must give to her daughter
a box, sturdy and solid.
No matter the material, stone,
clay, wood,
woven flax.

And if a woman should grow
without her own,
then she should craft the tools
and then build it of herself,
to protect her precious being.

And this box, without a key,
should be kept in the deep recesses,
the far corners of the heart,
where no stray hands might wander,
wrong intents defile.

Yes, every mother must remind her daughter
of the dignity inside,
the strength that helps her lift her chin
and keeps her voice firm,
an unwavering spark.

And if a woman should grow without
the words that line her being,
that affirm her in herself,
then she must form them
and repeat,

soft as a mantra,
that in the midst of everything,
her box might bear the buffeting,
and she might stand, counted
on her own foundation.

And strong,
as flax bends in the wind.

April 15 – Northern Hemisphere
October 16 – Southern Hemisphere

Water of Life

Ah, there are two ways of writing.

One, to come to it educated,
so you know the literary forms
and the tricks,
the ever twirling hoops.

And have read
the poets with the accolades,
the authors with the little big letters
after pen names.

The other is to come,
a student of no formal learning,
but with a heart and pen open,
held loosely in the palm.

Remembering the day
you first fell so unexpectedly,
and then like love
were entirely consumed.

So that now you could not get up
from the well's floor,

for the simple matter of
needing to survive –

poetry as it is,
being manna from heaven
and the ever-flowing water
of life.

The Weight of Water

It's how we live,
like poetry.

We start with a word,
maybe two,

but not so many
that the flow is restricted.

And then we follow
the constant thread,

as a river looks
for the lowest point,

or as blossoms open
under a warming sun.

There is nothing
that looks too much like force.

Have you ever picked the rose
bud

and hoped it might
come to bloom in the vase?

No, there is nothing about
trying too hard.

More,
it's like free fall.

Like trusting in wings
we cannot see,

making the undefinable
visible.

There is someone
speaking in our ear in tongues,

we listen though
we mightn't understand.

It's almost as though that part
is of the least import.

It's the child in us
that possesses the Kingdom.

And instead
of rising in knowledge,

we rest upon
the weight of water,

carving out its path
to the sea.

The Artists Teach Us

The artists teach us
that a canvas isn't blank.

That what they paint
has already long appeared in the mind.

For them it becomes simply
tracing lines of a thought,

like a stream is followed
to the outlet of the sea.

The artists teach us
that an empty page is far from fixed.

That materials and techniques aside,
what matters is

awareness
of what is always taking shape,

that the pen or brush might capture
and transcribe.

The artists teach us
that nothing's set in stone.
Rather anytime clouds might be brushed aside
to make way for sky,

and rough waters made smooth by the flick of the wrist,
or light all of a sudden appear.

Yes, everything can change
and the artist holds a wand.

Knowing creation is happening all around
and our days are blank pages,

and doors we enter in,
to look around and see what we might see.

And perhaps more than that,
they are framed spaces in which we move,

or like a labyrinth
might trace under feet.

Love Because

Today I need the peace of quiet things.
The beauty to remind me I'm worthy.

The beauty of God's signature.
The letter without words, framed with the view.

Worthiness comes and goes
according to feeling, or memory.
But the peace of quiet things,
the beauty unadorned,

but which forever greens outside the window
is a gift without the earning.

Not an afterthought
but a promise, signed and sealed.

Expressed in the way the earth renews
with its green covering.

Beauty teaches, everything that's worthy
lies fertile for growth.

Beauty given without expectation of return
is more than a gracious gift.

It is love because,
just because we are enough,

even lying here in the dark.

Yes, today I need the peace of quiet things.
The emerging green.

The way the grasses hit the sunlight,
the seed-laden shafts ripe with next season's gain.

Yes, everything that lies fertile
is ripe yet for growth.

Beauty, which is God's signature,
and the letter without words framed with a view

gives us our entitlement.

A crown of leaves
inset with seed-studded jewels.

Praise in the Morning

This morning I woke with praise on my lips
in the half-conscious state
that breaks upon us before the light.

I lay there aware how praise
made up the lining of my soul's walls
in this world in which I reside.

And truer than the life lived in
the light of day,
I know it's these half-breathed prayers,

this worship uninhibited by awareness,
these entreaties whispered to an ear
when hardly conscious of my speech,

that is heard and acted upon.

This morning
the song that sprang from my lips
in the fading dark

spoke of the wonders my spirit knows
and would remind me of
in each day's awakening.

And I'm aware how, when
I take these moments into the day,
they become a staff to open the sea before me.

Yes, this life that makes no sense
without the soul's communion
and the heeding of God's voice

becomes a wide way through the parting waves
when the Spirit leads.

April 20 - Northern Hemisphere
October 21 - Southern Hemisphere

Shine

I got up with the birds today.
The heavy cloak that covered me as I slept
tucked its edges around me
that for a moment I could not breathe,

could not sense the light
for the dark –
lifted with the birds.

The birds whose morning song
tore the curtain
and opened the tomb,

as though the light had always
been waiting in the wings.

I got up with the birds today,

who recalled to me
how darkness might threaten
to veil our faith and joy,

but that song is a tonic for our pains
and griefs.
And fears that threaten with their dark edge

are simply covers that we remove
as we rise and stand
and claim the light of day

to chase away
the vestiges of the night.

I got up with the birds today.

And took with relief a big expansive breath
as I remembered
how light shines from without and within.

That the dawn that rises in the east before my eyes
ascends also in my heart
to burst at its seams.

Like the sun that will soon
crest the clouds to flood the sky,
I am reminded to shine from inside out

and sing as though I'd always had a song
ready, like the birds,

to greet the day.

April 21 – Northern Hemisphere
October 22 – Southern Hemisphere

How to Know

How to know God?
Stop to breathe,
sink like a stone into the silence
from which all sound comes.

Then travel and follow
the voice of the birds,
the waves on the sea,
the brush of branches in the wind.

All activity
arising from its origins in the wellspring,
the storehouse of energy.

And stop, close the eyes,
see how the dark is a comfort,
like the womb
and its near beating heart.

This womb,
which in turn becomes
a passage to the light,
to stun in all its brightness.

And this light, a dance of electrons
absorbing energy to throw off,
return to their orbit.

So, how to know God?
Gather in the facts,
others still beside,
attempt to understand and see how

the colours shown are perceived
only by the colour reflected,
the apple green for it being
the shade unabsorbed –

proving there is always more we cannot know,
what we see even, dependent on our vision.

And then sink,
like a stone does without any hearing,
or return like a child in the womb
without knowledge,

or as electrons throwing off light
and then returning to their orbit,
their cloud surrounding the atom's central heart.
Yes, how to know

what can't be known?
Give in, open your eyes.

April 22 - Northern Hemisphere
October 23 - Southern Hemisphere

Rise

I give up
all that isn't me,
although tomorrow I know
I will try for it to be retrieved.

But for today
I give up what isn't mine to carry
or feel the weight of upon my heart
as if my name were engraved.

Yes, today I give up all that attempts
to harness the mind,
and the spirit loosed
can then float as is meant.

As a leaf glides on the river,
or birds soar on the air,
the currents of life
need our gracious bearing.

Heads held high,
eyes centered on what's ours,
letting go the things
God has never fashioned.

Yes, today I discard all that isn't me.
And I find myself afresh
in the freedom
of its shedding.

As today I lay down the weights
that would hamper my rise,
and realise again
how close is heaven.

This

When you can say
I do not know why
this joy,

your happiness will take wings
and climb and climb,
not dependent on restraint,

to where the dancing clouds
catch the first beams of light.

Joy has as little need to comprehend a why
as we do to know
the reasons for being.

The naysayers
who sit on the ground
sifting their wrongs and rights

hardly know
that there is this
here, right now,

this rising light.

Musings

I take my garden seat
and it's as though the conductor
opens the score just for me.

Or perhaps
it's that I've just broached
the moment unawares

and the bees and the tuis,
the passing gull against the blue,
see me but as colour in a collage,

or a pattern in a landscape,
or the backing of a symphony
if I were bold.

Although, more likely
I stand out
as something ill fit

but still blessed to steal a position
on the sidelines of a moment
dropped from heaven,

or rather,
an ever-present unfolding
when seen for what it is,

this commonplace,
with wonder mixed.

To the Sun

I am going to where I can see the sun

rise
and round and set.

To where the grass lays itself out
long and wide,

stretches to rest
in the lee of hills.

And rises to the roots of trees,
whose crowns in the sun's passing gaze

turn golden at their edge.

I am going to where the dew,

wet on the length of branches
catches the dawn

and glistens like a body
warm from love.

To where the world for a day

is lit up like a prize made
just for God.

And from which we might take a measure
for ourselves.

I am going home,

to where the world's turning years
recede,

to where the child in me
takes a hop and a step across hills

from my youthful self
to here.

To where I will give the years to God
and watch hurts dissolve as sun in mist.

And see joys lengthen out like fields,
growing as grass

new in spring.

Follow your Heart

Follow your heart,
it tends to leave prints wherever it goes,
as bare feet on frosty grass.

Trace back
to where impressions were made,
like etchings on wood or signs at crossroads.

Feel for the indents,
and then see which direction they point.
Eyes shut, let your heart take the lead.

Take the prayers you have not yet uttered.
Give them voice
and see the frames they make,

as houses yet to be lived in.
See how the words start to give them shape and substance,
walls and roof.

Like a garden,
see what recurring thoughts take root each season,
stay and grow, dispersing seed in the wind.

Listen to your heart.
It tends to stay
where it feels a need, or a welcome,

and then it calls you back,
echoing on the airwaves.
Naming your longings with your own voice.

Labyrinth

I walk the labyrinth to you.
Catching sight of your smile
as though across a room.

I make my way but
my feet are slow,
tied to the ground.

While you are there I realise I am far,
and the labyrinth that I walk
turns me away,

that I must cast
a look behind
to see your face.

And I must go back
to where I begin,
again.

But you're still there,
your gaze a beacon of light
in which I'm held.

And as I walk,
I realise both in shadow
and in sun,

this path is a spiral
leading on
though I might appear to retrace my route.

And my heart all the while
is safe in yours,
in this grace which surrounds.

And I see how
this centre I'm seeking,
this face I love

is my own looking back,
in the bosom
of your love.

The Heart has a Hole

The heart has a hole in it.

Just when we think we've had enough
that we might flood
and overflow,

the outlet at the heart
gives way,
releasing all its weight.

The heart has a tendency
towards resurrection,
beating its way back from death.

What feels as a wound to the core
finds salvation
in the way the heart holds space

for itself,
nurturing and restoring
anew from the inside.

The heart has a hole in it.

As all broken vessels are made stronger
by the way they're cracked
and repaired,

we do not know whose heart is whole
by looking,
but we know how hurt can serve a purpose.

And the heart that is whole
is the one that has bled
and sealed its tender parts

but left an outlet
for the overflow
and the pressure to subside.

There is always hope.
And the heart that is whole
looks out from itself

through the crevices of its shell
and shows a new compassion,
a new way of growing beyond its parts.

Love finds its way out.

What Takes Our Breath

Whatever takes our breath
tends to give it back threefold.

What stops the heart,
the things that take us unaware,

which cause our breath to pause
and lungs to hurt,

these sudden things
which wake us from our slumber,

whether of the sublime
or painful kind,

they are the things we remember
for how they shock us in our trajectory,

to turn us by degrees
and orient us someplace else.

Yes, whatever takes our breath
tends to return it again.

Like the heart that stops
to restart at medical intervention,

or the lump swallowed
when words are said and bombshells dropped,

or the grief that arrives
in the same instant beauty drops our defences,

knowing a lifetime is lived
between such moments.

Yes, whatever it is
that restarts the heart in its beating,

that causes our lungs to expand
and hold still for an infinite second,

they are the turns we make,
the petite morts,

or loss of consciousness
between one life and the next,

the little resurrections
to raise us up from our beds.

Bread

We are the bread of life.
Dropped crumbs for the hungry.

A warm yeast rising
to fill our place.

A swelling grace
that yields itself for others' nourishing.

We are bread that does not run out
but refills our plates.

And multiplies that none
lack sustenance.

We are bread.

We are the water of life.
Welling rivers for the thirsty.

A warm weight flowing,
giving at its edges,

expanding to fill the empty fissures
and wet the dry earth.

We are the water that ever springs,
liquid dressing to soothe wounds

and absorb the world's pain
in a rising flood.

We are water.
We are bread.

Givers of life.

May 1 - Northern Hemisphere
November 1 - Southern Hemisphere

Go

I'm waiting for a word, like 'Go'.
And realise,
'Go' has already been said.

'Go' has been said
since the earth rounded the sun
the first time.

And the earth has kept up momentum,
no matter
she might not know the goal.

'Go' has been said
since the heart first commenced
its beating.

Imagine this new organ still
until the first pump of blood.
And what impetus causes it to do what it's meant?

Oh, 'Go' has been said
that we don't need to hear its message clear
again and again.

Indeed any act that moves us
forwards, upwards, and out
is good.

For what has not yet been said
is 'Stop'.
'Rest' yes, like the animals and the seasons.

But while the earth moves
we can do so too,
no permission needed.

When the World Beckons

What do you do when the world opens,
curls her little finger to beckon?

What do you do when you see
a glimpse through the curtains,

or a sliver of blue
through parting clouds?

What do you do
when your heart quakes

and your feet adhere
to familiar rock?

What do you do?

Are opportune moments
always appearing,

or are they more like shooting stars,
one in a million?

What do you do?
How do you know

that this parting sea
is not just a mirage?

That when we throw ourselves into the red
we will not be cast out.

What do we do when the world beckons,
summoning with her hands?

What do we do
but lay down as children weaned,

flotsam
on the waves of the sea.

May 3 – Northern Hemisphere
November 3 – Southern Hemisphere

Talking About the Sun

My friends talk about the sun.
How it hangs and rises
and sets.
It is as though
this sun,
and its daily returning light,
is a deity by which
we see everything.

My friends capture
the sun,
in a word,
a camera's lens,
in a moment's paused breath.
It's as though this remembrance
is a piece of perfect,
to preserve as a record of good.

My friends point to the sun
and exclaim, 'Look'!
And we do, and consider how
perhaps more than one of us
are loved.
And maybe we each are worth

its radiant countenance
upon us.

If not today
then maybe tomorrow,
or next time we find ourselves
caught within its sights,
wooed by a glance
in this stolen moment.
The light rising and ascending
just for us.

Love is Stronger

Love is stronger.
Water is a drop
on its own,
insubstantial and as
ethereal as dew
fallen on grass.

Almost weightless,
its translucent form,
at half a gram,
hardly bears
our notice.

At a spit
we hardly register it,
a handful
we raise our face
to feel the grace of its caress.

Its pressure
finally gaining at
the onset of a shower,
at which we might
then unfold our shelter.

Love is stronger.

Water as a river,
its weight combined in force,
has the power
to carve out ravines
in mountains.

And water in a wave,
with its weight behind it,
is able over time
to break rocks
to smithereens.
Water, in its softness,
belies its very strength,
when with gentle touch
we feel it run
through fingers.

But water in abundance
has the power to awe
as we watch it
unfurl over rocks
in a waterfall.

Love is stronger.

Yes, love that mimics water
is in the snow,
whose weight breaks
the branches
of the pine.

And love that resembles
a river
is in the spring rains
that engulf the
thirsty land.

And love that overcomes
is in the kiss
of a mother goodnight,
multiplied
a million times.

And love that drives out dark
is in the wave that
bears the goodwill
of nations
behind it as a flood.

Faithful

I record God's faithfulness,
that when asked I might say,
whenever has a prayer gone unanswered,

a night not turned to day by itself,
a spring branch not borne its blossom,
or an autumn tree not divested its green.

Whenever has God not turned
with the seasons on a branch,
or a seed bursting in the earth for us.

Yes, I would show how, like the rings marked on a trunk,
or an earth rounding its sun,
God is ever intent upon our growth.

Ever drawing us as a plant towards the light,
or keeping us in gravity's pull,
a celestial body tracing its orbit.

Yes, I record God's faithfulness
so that when asked I can say,
whenever have prayers, voiceless or not,

not found a fertile place in God's earth to fall,
to be buried until the spring
of their fruition.

God is ever faithful as the sun, the source of light and life,
or as sap in the central branch of the vine,
that we might flourish

as burgeoning grapes upon its stem.

Thumb Print

It's more than being made
in God's image, thumbprint,
glory.

For so long I saw it
as an outer garment.

That God was here,
a man with feet and hands,
a heart that beats.

And thus are we.

But it stopped at skin.
This understanding,
at a physical defining line.

For how could God,
all good, all love,
be found in us?

Imperfect beings.

And then one day
the world opened up,
like a map unfolded.

And God was no longer
separate to the flesh
inhabited.

The singing in my head
and blood
was I and God in unison.

The veins,
all dripping light,
the heart attempting to love
was God imbibed
like mother's milk,
an endless stream.

Like gold etchings in a canvas,
God was here,
threaded through.

For what artist is ever dispassionate,
impartial to his design,
rather instead

the artist's soul is ever entwined
in each expression,
each particle of his making.

And creation is an endless
process of unfolding,
not unlike the way each day

the sky meets the sun,
paintbrush in hand.

Loose

Did this garden ask anything of me?

Planted, it only sought the light
and nourishment of life.

It only inclined towards the north
to where the sun burned warmest.

Without my taming solicitous hand
it grows and thrives.

And I stand blessed to watch,
and I stand small here, underneath.

Does life ask anything of us

that planted we don't already know
how to do?

This being doesn't take any
emerging talent.

We incline towards growth
as a natural, inevitable occurrence.

So watch the tamers and the solicitous,
and let God's world illustrate,

as it always has,
what life looks like

when let loose
to grow.

A Curtain

Time is a curtain drawn,

like this dressing of new leaves
upon the maple tree,
delicate thin
green veil,
which the wind whips and lifts
that the sky shows through.

And the future
and the past
seem to converge
at this axis
of trunk rising
like a solid sign of continuity –

branches pointing back
and forwards,
excepting that all is round, surrounding,
and we turn
to not know
forward from return.

Which we realise
is altogether well,

that at times the curtain's drawn,
delicate thin,
and the behind is the eternal thing
peeking through.

Yes,
at the axis
we can pick a branch
and follow through,
no matter which we take
there are the enduring things –

like veins in a leaf,
and green
of a hue that can only be described
as new, recurring, promising,
like spring looks
when the veil's pulled back.

And blue,
ever changing and encompassing,
as the sky
that spreads its blanket
wide
for catching falls.

Yes, there is a curtain drawn,

that we can trust the closing
and the opening,
and the direction,
though sometimes
we might turn
to lose all sense of navigation.

The winds whips
and lifts
the green leaves to dancing
like living,
moving sprites,
and the sun –

which now has burnished
the leaves gold
at their outer sides –
reminds us
of all the things
surrounding,

though we might not be sure
of forwards from return.

The Secret of the Acorn

Ah, the secret

is in the acorn that bursts,
is dropped
to grow a tree again.

The secret is often in
the smallest things
hidden in clear sight.

In the womb,
flesh and muscle,
the nourishment of blood,

a cocoon to grow
the secret things
to life.

Yes, the secret is in
how, when everything is ready,
life appears – surprise.

Yes, who might think,
seen in freeze frame,
the solid winter ground hid seeds.

But a seal is only there
for a turning season,
or until what is within pushes out.

The danger is to take
everything at face value,
the things that don't announce their presence.

But hope is the secret hid
under the smooth acorn's shell
and the melting snow's warming soil.

All that's hard and round,
or sealed,
points to a secret hidden.

The oyster shell
or jagged rock wall
at a cave's entrance.

Yes, the secret is in
how the acorn belies belief
at first sight.

But come again
and a tree has grown
right out of a shell.

Hope is in a fractured stone
giving way
to a new day.

Or a passageway appearing
all of a sudden,
shedding light on an empty floor.

Treasures

Treasures.

I will put them in my kete.
And I will be rich,
with a wealth of blossom,
the flushed cheek of dawn
and kiss of sun.

Memories
I've been too hungry
to put anywhere
and dreams too unformed yet
for shape.

All the residue
now melted down
and the elements
of future possibilities
carried safe in this basket of flax.

Yes, nature's provision
and the patient weaving
of another's hands,
whom I shall never meet,
has given me a forever gift.

Isn't that always
the way with treasured things.
Passed down,
prepared with prayer,
anointed with the love they come with.

Like the blossom on the tree
appearing every year,
the sun's rounding visit,
this remembrance of things that
disappear to yet return.

We keep them in our kete.
We take them out to hold them
and are held again.

Rain from Heaven

I have a gift for you,
which, like all gifts held
in the width of two hands,
is greater than the sum of its weight.

I have a gift that I give without words,
written or spoken.
Sometimes words do not bear the hearing
or adequately carry themselves clothed.

Instead, my gift is open,
like a vessel bearing treasure unguarded,
or a stream running
down an incline.

There is something stronger and greater even
than love,
which at its best can ask for an
exchange.

There is only one thing that is truly free,
for it not being merited or deserved even.
Grace comes ever flowing,
and mercy like the rain from heaven.

Tender

Stay tender,
hurt can be a friend,
softening the heart.

And the soft heart
has eyes and ears

to see and hear.
Sensitive to life.

And the tears that easily shed
are like rain,

that the fertile ground
melts to receive.

Stay true,
there is much to mar our dreams
of how life should be.

But the true heart
beats ever on

and learns that life, in seasons,
is for sowing,

for reaping,
and for storing our seed.

What does not strike today
may not yet have reached its time.

And the heart,
we learn the heart is like flesh
responding to touch.

We know what matters
by how much it echoes through us.

By how we shake
and shiver, and erupt

in response to the things that move,
and stir our passions.

So that we make dreams come to life
by first envisaging them.

Stay soft,
pliable,
ready to adapt.

Like water that ever springs,
then cuts its course to lowest ground.

Making a track
where it feels a give.

Yes, everything is sensitive
to everything else.

And everything returns,
like water, like life.

Pregnant

Space is not empty.
Space is pregnant with possibility.

The space we give each other,

the more expansive it is,
the more we are committed to preserving it,

the more the space gives room for flourishing,
the more a space gives a place for truth.

The more we allow each other a place
to grieve, to doubt,

to question, lament, and rant,
release and confess.

The more the space becomes a womb
from which new life is nurtured and birthed.

Space is not absence.
Space is not washing our hands of care.

Space is presence at its most attentive.
Space is love in response to need.

And this space we give each other,
out of preference and grace,

this space is made to grow its contents,
to bring to life what is yet being conceived.

No, space is never empty.

Whether blessed or devoid of empathy
it is a permeating presence.

A holy incubator
of germinating seeds.

And space that's pregnant with possibility,
sown with good intents,

becomes the means for life to be multiplied
and for truth to shed its protective sheath.

To stand naked and counted,
a voice in the wilderness growing in strength.

That life might bloom
and potential be reached,

and the Body birth
its sacred gifts.

Blooms Upon the Sidewalk

I am aware
of pain,
and poverty immeasurable.

I know
there are enough tears
to float a million ships.

Enough need to
turn our prayers
to silence.

I am aware of the 'O'
my lips make
when faced with truth.

The way my hands wring
and want to unburden themselves
of possession.

Alleviate this guilt,
the heavy heart
of the blessed rich.

But am I better
for what I give up?
Maybe.

But each of us I think
is given something greater
to give,

of more worth
than we can achieve
by denial.

Which is why I am aware
of pain
and poverty immeasurable.
The tears
that bear a million
ships upright.

The 'O' that causes my
heart to break in two
apart,

and pour out flowers
to float
on the waterways.

What is guilt alleviated,
compared to love
and joy unmasked.

The pain of this world
asks for our response,
and for some of us

it's to bring an antidote.
Beauty to ease
the weary heart.

To impart hope
where thought of hope
was lost.

As blooms
upon the sidewalk,
pointing to the sky.

At a Distance

And while he was still at a distance,
far back,
a father caught a glimpse

the way we might perceive someone once known
in a crowd
by the gait of their walk
or a long-familiar gesture

And then look again
with heart suspended,
weightless in our mouth,
hopeful and expectant.

Yes, while he was small against the hill,
the dust of the road
and shimmer of the afternoon
obscuring his view,

a father dropped his arm, raised into the sun
and ran,
overjoyed
from long seasons of waiting.

And likewise, we are called persistently
from hiding.

The flag of shame we think
stains red our skin
is the very hue
our father picks out far upon the hill,

that he knows now to ready for a
celebration,
knows now
heaven will join in welcome.

May 16 – Northern Hemisphere
November 16 – Southern Hemisphere

Child of God

Which of us would not want to say,
as the woman at the well,

'I met a man who told me of everything I had done.'

There are those who see us
from inside out,
straight past the skin,

who trace patterns on our undersides,
that we need not wear pretence
as a shield,

can pour ourselves,
as water gains momentum
and runs clear.

I met a man who told me
at once who I was,
loved child of God.

That like a river
that breaks its dam,
I might begin to flow.

There are those who see
who we are
and love us still.

That we might ask,
'Was that the Christ
in shepherd's clothes?'

Yes,
compassion is the gift that
makes us most like God,

that those held
in its gaze
might claim healing long arriving.

Which of us wouldn't want to say,
I met a man
with whom I could stand bare,

that on my skin
he might recall to me
my name.

The Temple

We come

and the angels are clearing the road,
for we come bearing treasure.

We come with bare feet and hands,
hardly aware of what it is we carry.

Vessels of clay
with our holy consignment.

Re-dignified
and exhorted to raise our heads,

we breathe
and feel our ribs,

temple of the living Spirit,
expand to give room.

We come

and carry ourselves
with a different carriage.

Part dust and part bearers
of the divine eternal spark.

We remember of whom we are made,
to whom we belong.

Whom we hold,
this holiness encased in skin.

Our body, even,
a thing of wonder and awe.

In its clay
and its brokenness,

for we carry home the temple
of the Lord.

No Word

No word is wasted.
The prayers spoken,
the heart's unwinding,
nothing is said in vain,
though the answers seem lacking.

No word is without a hearing,
no voice without an inclined ear
receiving its pourings,
its truths and its delusions,
its fears and pleas.

No word is without a considered response,
though we mightn't know it.
The whole universe is tasked
with orchestrating what is good for us,
that we might have life to choose at each crossroad.

No word is lost.
No word that lives for a moment
without its angels to carry it,
to proffer it forward
as a message of great import.

No word less than,
that it can't be preserved
forever before God,
an open case,
until it's established

or has fulfilled its purpose.
Or had its questions answered
or needs received
and housed in residence
as welcome guests.

Until the meaning for their
questions,
or their presence, answers itself.
No word comes back empty,
as each one counts.

The Body

It is said
that we cannot move
or breathe
without some wind
stirring a star somewhere.

I think that must be
how prayer works.
That in the moment
that I conjure you up,
your help is on its way.

Perhaps a bit like rumours spreading,
a bird might tell an angel,
whose wings then brush a star
that the star might give a little nudge
to God.

Yes, that might work
if we think of God as
somewhere on a cloud.
Which of course he is,
just as angels are up there brushing wings.

But God, who is within and out
has also set up house
within the heart,
and this Body
called a Church.

And the Body that moves
is a little like an ocean
propelled by the moon's
swelling.
It is sensitive to everything.

So that the pain you feel
is like a prod to my heart
and a cause for prayer
God has already heard
in the ears attached to us both.

Yes, something like the
concept of the wind
and the star,
and the breath that breathes
through the both of us.

So comforting to know
that this God within
and without
makes his body both in us
and the world.

And so you are part of me
as we are a part of God,
and everything that has

atoms even,
or breath.

And prayer –
well, prayer becomes something
not so hard to understand
when we conceive of
the myriad of threads.

Back

You took me back.

Back
with your love.

Back until there was no space
between us.

Back, back
a thousand million years

and counting.

Back,
falling in time,

wind
in my ears,

from the cross
to the garden.

To a garden
where we walk

like the world is new
and fresh,

untainted yet
by the things

to bring me shame.

And our love
is full of promise.

Like a new earth on
the cusp,

and eternity
just beginning.

Only you can take me
back,

the broken
made whole.

Disgrace
far removed,

as sins crossed out
in the sand.

And the garden,

the garden
where we walk

restored, as though
darkness never were.

This cross the eraser of all
to separate us.

You take me back.

May 21 – Northern Hemisphere
November 21 – Southern Hemisphere

The Middle

My right on one side and yours on the other.
And God walks down the middle
carrying sheaves.

My right is on one side and yours so far
I cannot contemplate it
without seeming to give up my view.

But God walks down the middle,
the author of the Word,
shedding seeds as grain yet to grow.

My right is here and yours so wrong appearing
that I wonder if our saviour
is the same?

Does God look different on your side
as to mine,
or is it that we see the face we seek?

But God strides down the middle,
smiling to himself,
as he walks bidding us to follow.

Speaking in Verse

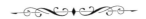

It's a day of poetry,
this day we speak in verse.

But every day is a day for poetry.
Even the days we have lost
all forms of speech.

When the silence in us expands
that our voice when we go to seek it,
we find abandoned.

Lost for words and waiting,
like waiting for a morning
so long in coming.

Like waiting for hope,
hope which,
like poetry,

comes in sheaves
of written words
and empty pages

through which we read for meaning
between the lines,
searching for what we need to see.

That poetry,
the illusive lover,
the heart's muse,

would be the thing we need
day after day
to paper over the cracks,

to staunch the flow of tears,
to bandage the hurt places –
is the miracle of verse.

That it would be the thing
that makes us wait,
hopeful,

like those
for whom the sun once rose
that they know it will again.

And faithfully, even when
the tongue is mute
or still like a mouth in sleep.
For when did poetry ever need
the words
to speak,

and when did hope
ever need speech
to come dressed

like a morning
reappearing.

Questions

Why the hurry
and the angst?
The questions making tracks
to circle upon themselves.

What is not complete,
answered, clarified,
will in a flash too quick for thought
be understood.

The pieces that now exist
separate in pockets and drawers
with ill-fitting edges
that they have no partners

will find their place
without our help,
that the map will have no
dark place yet undiscovered.

The things we reach for now
into the abyss
and keep the remembrance in our heart
will one day emerge into profile.

And while we wait,
we remember how
we are already found,
right here where we're meant to live.

Dreaming has its place,
and longing points to spaces
we're to fill
with the things we can reach out and touch.

To love what's given us,
knowing God has a way of wrapping safe
contents not intact,
that we can trust what exists yet incomplete.

And perhaps, in the day of restoration
and revelation,
we might see what mattered most
in the shedding of light upon truth.

That those things of real import
were the matters in our hands taking shape,
that in that day
we might be another's puzzle complete.

Stories

My story is woven in your story.
Because our paths crossed,
connected, carried on in step,
diverged,

I have become a bigger story.

If we are each of us streams,
then the place we flow into each other
is our rushing river, our brimming over,
our rich heritage.

We have become a grateful history.

And the place we flow out of each other
to put down sweet roots,
our offshoot from the branch, our fertile bush –
our turangawaewae –

is where we stand separate but together.

I am glad to be in this river with you.
Your blessing is my drink,
my sustenance your pleasure, twin streams
in differing directions.

We become a waterway of many branched
tributaries.

Our stories intertwining, dividing,
becoming bigger.

'Turangawaewae'
A Place to Stand
(our place of belonging, sacred spiritual place)

May 25 - Northern Hemisphere
November 25 - Southern Hemisphere

East Cape
– a Remembrance –

When we rounded the corner
I lost all sense of language,

at each bend
the only response attentiveness,

silence.

Which perhaps does not explain
the eruption of excitement,

the shifting in my seat
to not miss any long length

of coast, rise of bush,
stretch of sea.

Perhaps the awe
was best said in flustered

scurrying for paper, pen.

Exclaiming all the while,
'the beauty, the beauty'.

I remember now
how we stopped at the edge,

the turn around the hill,
the ocean spread

out like a cloak of many
colours,

that my heart rose up
inside my mouth,

my soul dropped
to the floor

of my stomach,
my breath exhaled.

My spirit held me up.

'The beauty, the beauty.'

'E whitia ana au e te rā'
'I am being shone on by the sun.'

The Key

For those in love with love,
poetry is the key.

The essential element to living.

The need that arises again
after the ingesting,

which keeps us returning.
Feeling

our way as a people
bereft of sight,

until the objects of our affection
orbit again into our vision.

We are like over-imbibers
frequenting a tavern's door,

or lovers whose restless longings
have them turning circles,

revolutions
of gratification and recurring need,

as waves
that polish the beach,

to be pulled back by the moon
too soon.

Poetry is the key
turned

like a love consummated,
only to resume its pursuit again

from the beginning,
as dance steps on repeat.

Yes, for those in love with love,
poetry is the key.

But not the end.

Not so long
as there is more to receive

of poetry
and of love.

Ah Poetry

Ah poetry,
who would take another lover
who has poetry to softly
whisper sonnets
into their open ear.

To fall upon the face of
and give in
to the moving waves,
as though poetry
were a door to heaven.

Who would want
otherwise
when poetry
is both emotion
and emotion's relief.

To those for whom poetry
is the lover
and the beloved,
the expression and silent receipt
of some sacred gift –

poetry is
inexpressible comfort
and fuel to the flame
that burns within,
a voracious wick.

Ah poetry,
who would take another lover
who has poetry to softly
whisper sonnets
into their open ear.

To fall upon the face of
and give in
to the moving waves,
as though poetry
were a door to heaven.

Your Table

God, all of us, sinners and saints
come to you for bread.

Who's to know whose lips are chaste,
who is holy to touch your robe,
to entreat your ears.

But you hear,
and you allow the least of us a place at the table to talk,
to plead our case.

And your robe is grasped at most by the crowds at your feet.
All of us, sinners and saints,
that on a good day who would see the difference?

Even the least of us in love with you enough
that your glory rubs off,
and full of gratefulness that your mercy enters deep.

And the holiest amongst us might not know to bow their heads,
nor to pour perfume upon your head,
wash your feet –

with their arguing still where to sit.

A Gift

The things you have for us,
we are sometimes too afraid to open.

Fearful of this bright shining passage
to the sea.

Although we hear the gulls
in our imagination,

and picture the sails catching the wind
on the horizon,
we fear the things you have for us
are too daunting,

too good
that we are wary.

As those who might retreat
back from the fire's heat,

we do not want our fingers
burnt.

But the things you have for us
are not without due preparation.

What giver would only beautify
the wrapping?

It's the gift beneath
to which you give your full attention.

That we might open
and find ourselves in the receiving.

And walk with you
the bright shining passage

to the sea.

Benediction

Burn off, burn off
like the coming of the light.
Leave yesterday in a blaze of leaves.
Pile of ashes.

Today is always a revolutionary turn
to the east.
To watch how the sun brings
every dark corner to light.

Each day naked as Adam and Eve
we walk in the garden astonished.
That we are given another day
is always amazing.

We, children fresh from bed
whose mother has tenderly clothed us.
Souls whose sun has dawned
to speak of resurrection.

That each leaf lit by a flame
becomes less a
a singular feature
than a living body, glowing.

We are fused back into the vine.
As parishioners gathering
at an altar,
receiving their daily grace.

Come Singing

Lord, let us come singing,
remembering who we are.
Branches of the vine
bearing spring to one another.

Lord, let us come loving,
forgetting what we are not,
for griefs do not define us
and joy responds to joy.

Lord, let us come with gifts,
the wonder of yourself,
whose image and inestimable name
we carry within ourselves.

Lord, let us come expectant.
Although we bring you with us,
we also await your presence
and the treasures to be unveiled.

Lord, let us come humbly.
It's only when we acknowledge our failings
that you reveal in us the power
of the resurrected one.

Lord, let us come together.
There is nothing to match the beauty
of a body that claims each part
as essential as the other.

So let us come singing,
remembering who we are –
branches of the vine
bearing spring to one another.

CPSIA information can be obtained
at www.ICGtesting.com
Printed in the USA
BVHW021454190821
614776BV00001B/1